Touching and feeling

Author's Note

I have worked alongside young children for more than forty years. Over this period I have learned never to be surprised at their perceptive comments about the physical world in which they live. Many of their observations ('Have you seen the crinkles in the elephant's trunk?' 'How do seeds know which is their top and which is their bottom?') indicate keen observation and an intuitive use of the senses of taste, touch, sight, smell and hearing.

The sense-dependent nature of the young child should come as no surprise to parents and teachers. In the early years of life images provided by the senses shape our interpretation of our surroundings and lay the foundations upon which subsequent learning is built. The ideas of hot and cold, far and near, quiet and loud, sweet and sour, soft and hard are developed through the interaction of the child with his or her immediate environment. This interaction encourages observation and questioning which in turn leads to talk and the extension and deepening of language.

This book (like its companions in the series) is a picture book which seeks to encourage both looking and talking. The text may be read by child or adult. Alternatively it may be ignored, the pictures alone being used to trigger an exploration of the child's own insights.

© Franklin Watts 1997
Franklin Watts
96 Leonard Street
London EC2A 4RH

Franklin Watts Australia
14 Mars Road
Lane Cove
NSW 2066

ISBN: 0 7496 2573 2

A CIP catalogue record for this book
is available from the British Library.

Dewey Decimal Classification Number: 612.8

10 9 8 7 6 5 4 3 2 1

Editor: Helen Lanz
Art Director: Robert Walster
Designer: Kirstie Billingham
Picture Research: Sarah Snashall

Printed in Malaysia

Picture credits

Commissioned photography by Steve Shott: cover, 4, 5.
Researched photography: Bruce Coleman Ltd 14
(P. Clement), 22 & 29 (J. Burton); Hutchinson Library
17 (L. Taylor); The Image Bank 7 (H. de Lespinasse), 8
(G. Obremski), 9 (R. M. Horowitz), 26-27 (I. Royd),
31 (D. W. Hamilton); James Davis Photography 12-13;
Robert Harding Picture Library 18 (G. Hellier), 20;
Franklin Watts title page; Zefa 10, 11, 15, 19, 23, 25
(K&H Benser).

Touching and feeling

by Henry Pluckrose

W

FRANKLIN WATTS

LONDON • NEW YORK • SYDNEY

We touch things with our hands
and our bodies.
The sense of touch
helps us to understand
the world in which we live.

Some things feel dry
and rough to touch . . .
like the crumbling surface
of an old wall,
or sand dried by the sun.

Some things feel smooth . . .
polished wood,
stones and pebbles
rounded by the sea,
the speckled shell
of a hen's egg.

Some things are soft
to the touch . . .
cats' fur, cotton wool,
a cuddly toy.

Some things are hard
to the touch.
Why do we use hard materials to
build our houses, schools,
factories and shops?

Some things are painful
to touch . . .
the prickles of the holly,
thorns on rose stems,
the needle-sharp hairs
of a cactus.

People who are blind
are taught to read
through their sense of touch.
They feel the raised shapes
on the paper with
the tips of their fingers.
The shapes form letters,
words and phrases.

We all use our fingers to read.
Our sense of touch
tells us if something is hot
or cold, rough or smooth,
soft or hard.

Imagine. If you touched
these things,
what would your hands
tell you?

What things do you
most enjoy touching . . .
the soft, squashy feel
of play-dough,
or the wet, slimy feel
of finger paints?

Perhaps you like the feel
of things which move,
touching you
when you touch them . . .
running water,
a friendly animal,
a cool wind on a hot day.

We use our sense of touch
to give messages . . .
a mother cuddles her baby
and each feels the other's love;
we shake hands to greet a visitor;
we kiss to say hello or goodbye.
We touch to give comfort.

This girl can feel the water
and sand all over her body.
People who are badly injured in
an accident may be able to see
what is touching them,
but not feel it.

Nearly all animals
have the sense of touch.
These puppies' eyes have
not yet opened.
They cannot see their mother,
but they feel the warmth
and comfort of her body.

Often our senses
work together.
We feel the wet
sea breeze in our face.
We may hear, taste,
see and smell it too!

Investigations

This book has been prepared to encourage the young user to think about the sense of touch. Each picture spread creates an opportunity for talk. Sharing talk with a sympathetic adult plays an important part in the development of a child's understanding of the world. Through the subtlety of language, ideas are formed, questioned and developed.

The photographs and supporting text concentrate on experiences common to most children - the softness of cats' fur, the cold, slimy feel of hand paints, the smoothness of glass or pebbles, the roughness of a tree's bark.

The theme of touch might be explored through questions and activities like these:

⭐ Encouraging a child to explain how things 'feel' in words makes a significant contribution to his/her language development. A simple way of uniting touch and language is through a 'feely bag' - a cloth with a pull-string opening. Into the bag (and unseen by the child) put a variety of small objects, e.g. a metal key, a coin, a scrap of fabric, a wrapped sweet, a plastic comb. Invite the child to put his/her hands into the bag and to describe each object in turn. What are they made of? What are they used for? What gave you the clue to their use? How many things can you say about the objects just by touching them? What things can't you tell about them? This game can be played many times - though its long term success depends on finding objects which intrigue.

⭐ Discussion could include the concept that the sense of 'feeling' also involves things that the child cannot see or touch directly – like warmth from sunlight.

⭐ Another important aspect of the sense of touch is that it does not only relate to hands – the whole of the body is touch-sensitive.

⭐ The way our senses work together can also be explored. What do we see that tells us that the frozen peas will feel cold to touch or that the water running into the bath is hot? If we can see heat and cold, can we also 'smell' heat, 'taste' cold – or hear them?